FROM ME TO YOU: THE SONG OF MY SALVATION

PRISCILLA L. ROSE

Copyright © 2021 KDC Publishing

All rights reserved.

ISBN: **978-0-692-13866-3**

First Printing 2021

Printed in the United States of America

Published by KDC Publishing
Chicago, IL

Unless otherwise indicated, scriptural quotations are taken from the King James Version of the Bible.

All Rights Reserved: All rights reserved under International Copyright Law. Written permission must be secured from the publisher to use or reproduce any part of this book, except for brief quotations in critical reviews or articles.

FROM ME TO YOU: THE SONG OF MY SALVATION

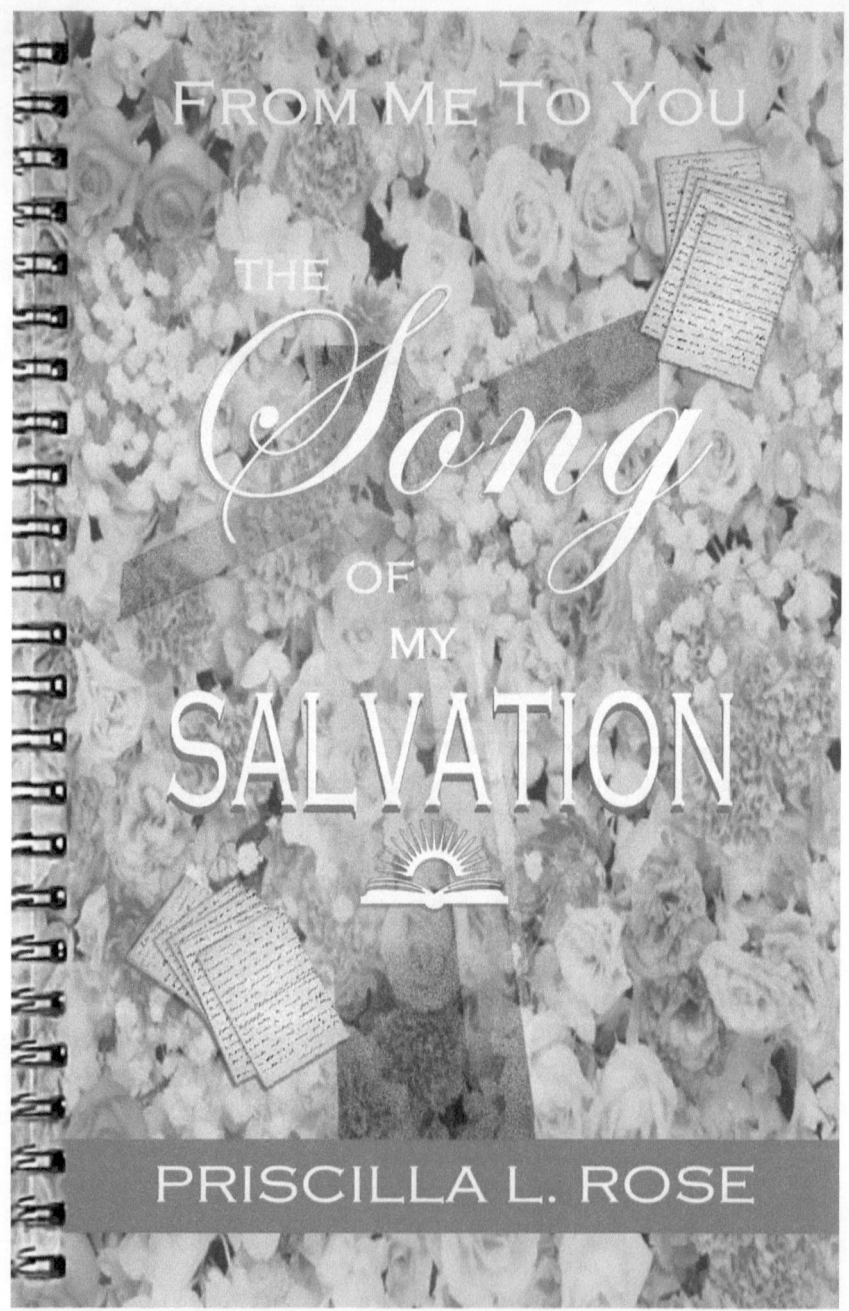

PRISCILLA L. ROSE

FROM ME TO YOU: THE SONG OF MY SALVATION

Dedication

Oh my, what a joy in serving the Lord!

I would like to take this time to dedicate and render this book back to my friend and counselor, the Holy Spirit; for it was Him who saw me through. Also, I want to thank Him for comforting me through every tear that was dropped and every laugh that was laughed.

Next, I would have to say thanks and I love you to the Women of God who spoke into my life and encouraged me to move forward: Evangelist Valarie Smith, Evangelists Paulette (RIP) and Pamela Harris.

Also, to my big sisters - Deborah Rose and Hope Brandon - whose testimonies kept me in check along the way (lol)!

~my prayer-warrior niece Natasha Rose for her endless encouragement and prayers.

~my big-brother cousin, Pastor Kerwin Modest - you already know.
~my grown babies Sarai and Zaire who also encouraged me along the way. Just know that It's Already Done! To God be the Glory!

PRISCILLA L. ROSE

FROM ME TO YOU: THE SONG OF MY SALVATION

TABLE OF CONTENTS

Dedication vi

Chapter 1
The Heart Is A Sensitive Matter (Zeal)

1. A Ready Heart 4
2. The Captivated Heart 7
3. Look No Further 10
4. Forever Thankful You're Not Man 13
   Poem: Truth 16

Chapter 2
Search My Soul Lord (Breaking)

5. This Way To Baggage Claims Please 20
6. By and By We Understand 23
7. A Place Called Stuck (In My Mind) 26
8. Hide Me Lord 29
9. And What Chocolate Did You Choose 32
10. So Why Did You Eat The Fruit 35
    Poem: Saved and Satisfied 38

Chapter 3
And My Eyes Shall See (Faith)

11. What Do You See? 44
12. Watchman! Watchman! What Does The Lord Say? . 47
13. In That Order 50
14. Roll Call Please 53

15. When Your Back Is Up Against The Wall 56
    Poem: Dusty Road 59

Chapter 4
Made Up Mind (Value)

16. My First I Shall Abide 64
17. Hidden Figure 67
18. Beauty For Ashes 70
19. Found Treasure 73
20. He Keeps His Promises 76
    Poem: Yes This Is For His Glory 80

Chapter 5
It's Mine (Joy)

21. Follow The Breadcrumbs .86
22. The Clean Up Is Real 89
23. So Fresh So Clean 92
24. Perfection We Go 96
25. Going For Broke 100
    Poem: Looking Beyond That Mountain 103

Chapter 6
Time To Shift (Levels)

26. Lead Me From The Dry Brook 109
27. Leap Baby Leap 114
28. Cross The Finish Line 118
29. My Color Of Peace 121
    Poem: No Way Of Return 124

PRISCILLA L. ROSE

FROM ME TO YOU: THE SONG OF MY SALVATION

Chapter 1
The Heart Is A Sensitive Matter
(Zeal)

1. *A Ready Heart*   4

2. *The Captivated Heart*   7

3. *Look No Further*   10

4. *Forever Thankful You're Not Man*   13

   Poem: Truth   16

PRISCILLA L. ROSE

FROM ME TO YOU: THE SONG OF MY SALVATION

1 A Ready Heart

> *And Zacchaeus stood, and said unto the Lord: Behold, Lord, the half of my goods I give to the poor; and if I have taken any thing from any man by false accusation, I restore him fourfold. And Jesus said unto him, This day is salvation come to this house, for so much as he also is a son of Abraham.*
> **Luke 19:8-9(KJV)**

It amazes me how Zacchaeus never questioned Jesus about how he knew his name and how he knew he was up in the tree. I assume it didn't dawn on him to ask because he was so excited and overwhelmed at the fact that, out of all the people that were there, he called his name and wanted to come to his house.

He didn't hesitate or procrastinate. He moved quickly to receive Jesus's call.

This should be our attitude when coming before the Lord: not slow to move, and without hesitation.

We should want to keep our zeal no matter what storm or valley we're going through; and, remember to always answer His call to prayer and supplication.

A ready and broken heart, and a yielded mind and soul is the only way we can receive what He has for us.

Open your heart to the Holy Spirit and allow Him to do the work in you and clean up those wounds and scars in your soul. Do not let the enemy block you from hearing the Lord's call for your healing.

Let the Holy Spirit unclog your ears and remove the scales so you may receive with a ready heart. Come to the operating room of deliverance and get your procedure done because He is calling us higher.

We cannot be weighted down with a heavy heart of depression or the feeling of being misunderstood.

Always keep in mind that God will call you first and that's the call that we should answer for He is always looking for a ready heart.

~ Amen

FROM ME TO YOU: THE SONG OF MY SALVATION

PRISCILLA L. ROSE

2 The Captivated Heart

I therefore, the prisoner of the Lord, beseech you that ye walk worthy of the vocation wherewith ye are called,
(Ephesians 4:1)

I once stood before You with a heart of stone; with a cold, stony heart of malice; filled with anger and confusion. Hurt and depression owned me and took residence in me. Lust whispered and told me that there is no other way.

Overtaken by the darkness of this world and the substance it offered me, I saw no way out and felt that hope was not within my grasp.

I fought the attacks of satan's imps that tried to suffocate me and steal my soul; but, I yelled out the only name I know that has the power and authority: JESUS!

I have gathered and gained so much until I refuse to take any more losses in my life. Trying my best not to put on the spirit of Lot's wife, for there is no time to look back.

Feeling the sigh of relief and freedom in my soul and taking back what the enemy stole.

At liberty is where you will catch me living until my Father calls me home. I had to find this place of rest in the Lord.

See, if you wrap yourself in the prison shackles and chains of love through Christ, you will understand who you are. You will also know that this walk is done in peace and unity in the Spirit of Him.

Not comparing yourself to others and the abilities the Holy Spirit

FROM ME TO YOU: THE SONG OF MY SALVATION

has graced them with. You will understand that the race is not given to the swift, but to you because you have fallen in love with Christ Jesus.

It's a love that only you know for yourself by the experiences you had in your life's journey; your testimony of the pits that were dug for you, but you made it out.

There is no turning back now for my heart has been captivated!

~ Amen

PRISCILLA L. ROSE

FROM ME TO YOU: THE SONG OF MY SALVATION

3 *Look No Further*

Philip findeth Nathanael, and saith unto him, We have found him, of whom Moses in the law, and the prophets, did write, Jesus of Nazareth, the son of Joseph. And Nathaniel said unto him, Can there any good thing come out of Nazareth? Philip saith unto him, Come and see.
St. John 1:45-46 KJV

It simply amazes me how we look to people and different objects and projects trying to find happiness, making idols of them.

It is like we must keep our hands busy to occupy our mind and keep our thoughts in check; searching for that true happiness and fulfillment to satisfy our inner desire of just doing something.

Getting lost in this world that is moving at a fast pace, not realizing that we are listening but not hearing and doing what the Holy Spirit is asking us to do:

"Take a breath. Hear Me. Sit still. You're too busy doing nothing. Hearken to the call. Wake up when I tap you on the shoulder. Let me speak to you this brand new morning that I allowed to spring forth. See what I need you to see. Open your heart to Me and receive My words of love and instruction."

It baffles me how Christ came and fulfilled what was prophesied and they still did not believe. He healed the sick and raised the dead, and they still could not grasp the fact that He was the Savior. As the old saying goes "The proof is in the pudding." They saw it, heard it, and I am sure they felt it when the people were healed.

Never judge a book by its cover; or judge a person from where they come from.

PRISCILLA L. ROSE

When we judge, we might miss it. Inspect the fruit for we are all fruit inspectors as people of God. Eventually, that person's true self will manifest and you will see them for who they truly are.

For I Am He who will supply all your needs. Be still and know that I Am is here. I shall restore and mend your broken hearts. I Am He who will bless and not curse. I Am Lord and the watchman of your soul; so, look no further.

~ Amen

FROM ME TO YOU: THE SONG OF MY SALVATION

PRISCILLA L. ROSE

4 Forever Thankful You Are Not Man

But the Lord said unto Samuel,Look not on his countenance,or on the height of his stature;because I have refused him:for the Lord seeth not as man seeth;for man looketh on the outward appearance,but the Lord looketh on the heart.
                                                    1 Samuel 16:7

It tickles my soul when we as men and women of God have a carnal belief of what we think the Kingdom looks like. It is not up to us. Everything is according to His will and purpose of Kingdom accountability.

We get the notion in our little bitty minds on how it should look, and who is in and who is out, comparing different ministries and leaders to each other, not realizing that people have different mantles and different assignments in the Kingdom.

See! God knows the gifts, power, and authority that you hold and carry in or outside of your region. But, most importantly, He knows your heart and the intent of your heart. God made us in His image, and we are unique individuals; no two are the same.

We may have some ways in common, but we are all different in how He made us perfect in His eyes because He really sees us for who He created us to be His and pieces of him. It brings joy to my heart to know that I'm fashioned and made after my Creator.

Sad to say, but we as people forget that God is Omnipresent so He knows who is putting their time in and who is not. He also knows

FROM ME TO YOU: THE SONG OF MY SALVATION

the direction in which you are going to go and with whom you would connect yourself to. So, make sure you are not chasing after man, but chasing Christ.

Then, decide in your mind that you are going to put God first because He knows what is best for you. Our ideas do not compare to what He has in store for us; and the results will bear the fruit and harvest that should come forth from the decision of putting Him first.

It is all about God and Kingdom work here on earth until He calls us home. So, do not be anxious and worried about anything that God has prepared for you.

Measure the man and woman of God to the word; and, if they line up, then follow them.

~ Amen

PRISCILLA L. ROSE

FROM ME TO YOU: THE SONG OF MY SALVATION

Truth Is

Truth is, I'm nothing without You,
I've got to make it all about You.

Truth is, there is no way around You,
But, yet I've found You, chiseling my heart away.

Truth is, the scales have fallen,
My eyes are open, You must lead the way.

Truth is, Your love is amazing,
No not complicated
I'm glad You are here to stay.

Truth is, I know you will not walk away.
Your glory is here to fill this place;
No more empty space.

Truth is, I know I'm the apple of Your eye
So glad to say
I'm Your ride or die.
Truth is, Your fragrance is grand.

PRISCILLA L. ROSE

Please take my hand
And help me to dismantle the enemies' plans.

Truth is, You are not man.
You have a master plan.
Truth is, You are sincere and perfect,
And I can go on for days.

But, the truth is, You are Truth,
And I love Your ways.

FROM ME TO YOU: THE SONG OF MY SALVATION

PRISCILLA L. ROSE

Chapter 2
Search My Soul Lord
(Breaking)

5. This Way To Baggage Claims Please   20

6. By and By We Understand   23

7. A Place Called Stuck (in my mind)   26

8. Hide Me Lord   29

9. And What Chocolate Did You Choose   32

10. So Why Did You Eat The Fruit   35

Poem: Saved and Satisfied   38

FROM ME TO YOU: THE SONG OF MY SALVATION

5 This Way To Baggage Claims, Please

But it displeased Jonah exceedingly, and he was very angry. And he prayed unto the Lord, and said, I pray thee, O Lord, was not this my saying, when I was yet in my country? Therefore I fled before unto Tarshish: for I knew that thou art a gracious God, and merciful, slow to anger, and of great kindness, and repentest thee of the evil. Therefore now, O Lord, take, I beseech thee, my life from me; for it is better for me to die than to live.

Jonah 4:1-3 (KJV)

Isn't it funny how we are swift to call out someone else's shortcomings or downfalls; better yet, their sin? Yet, despite ours, the Lord loves us, and forgives us, and allows us the opportunity to get it right.

It is not for us to say whom we believe the Lord should and should not forgive, or whom He should and should not bless.

Jonah was dealing with the spirit of disappointment and discouragement in dealing with the people of Nineveh. He was speaking the word, but no one would listen.

Sounds familiar, people of God?

Whether or not you are received, do not let the spirit of discouragement consume you. Do not be so quick to give up on your assignment. Let the Holy Spirit release you.
When you allow the Holy Spirit to release you, you will not prematurely drop your assignment.

PRISCILLA L. ROSE

Keep in mind, it is not about you; it's about what the Holy Spirit wants to do in the people and for the people. If you move in the spirit and not in flesh, you won't be bothered if people will receive the word or not.

Yes, it will grieve you because you want everyone to get it and not miss the mark. But, I'm sorry to say, it does not always work out like that. But know that God has the final say.

Jonah was moving in his flesh. However, I do believe that he started out with his heart in the right place. But, as time moved on, he got discouraged and felt the need to not complete his assignment.

If we look at the number of people or the amount of money, we will miss it – God will give the increase. All we have to do is keep the intent of our heart in right standing before Him and the people.

Let us remember that the people belong to the Lord, and this is who we are bringing them to. So, whether they receive you or not, give them what the Holy Spirit has given you to release no matter what.

For we wrestle not against flesh and blood. Please always keep this in mind and stay encouraged.

~ Amen

FROM ME TO YOU: THE SONG OF MY SALVATION

PRISCILLA L. ROSE

6 By And By We Understand

And we know that all things work together for our good to them that love God, to them who are the called according to his purpose
Romans 8:28

As we continue in Christ, the revelation of God's word starts to unveil. Our faith begins to grow and unlock different perspectives in us that we never knew existed. The word becomes enlightened to our soul and begins a healing and cleansing process.

This is when we can eat and digest the word without being spiritually "constipated." Now, we know that, when we are constipated, we are backed up, sick, frustrated and upset because our body needs to release.

But, we learn to just hold on and keep the faith, knowing that the Father does everything in His timing. Everything is already written in the books of heaven. But, there are some things that have to be put in perspective before we are able to handle certain responsibilities in the Kingdom.

So, do not get upset if it feels like things are not moving according to how you feel they should be moving. It is not up to us; it is according to His purpose. We have to keep that in mind.

Our desires may not be what He wants for us. He already knows the end results. So, let us keep our focus on Christ and everything else that we need will follow as long He is in our view.

If He called you to it, He will take you through it. His process

FROM ME TO YOU: THE SONG OF MY SALVATION

cannot be rushed unless He allows it. When we put our *two cents* in it, it causes delays in His plans.

So, remember that it is His will, and by and by you will understand.

~ Amen

PRISCILLA L. ROSE

FROM ME TO YOU: THE SONG OF MY SALVATION

7 A Place Called Stuck

(In my mind)

Let your conversation be without covetousness; and be content with such things as ye have : for he hath said, I will never leave thee, nor forsake thee.
                                                          Hebrews 13:5

Oh My God, how time has passed! We are in the 6th month, half of the year is gone and I feel like I am in a place called stuck. In my mind, nothing is moving in my life.

My flesh is getting impatient. *Will the words spoken prophetically come to pass?* Sigh...Be quiet flesh. I will not be moved by sight! I will not let the devil play that song of *"Eve trying to deceive me"* in my mind!

Again flesh, shake yourself and remind yourself that you shall hold on to every promise and every word that has been given by God's prophets, and the dreams and visions God has revealed unto me. Despite what it looks like and how things may sound right now, I am going to stand on every part of God's word.

I am going to call out those promises as I continue to move forward in God. I am going to remind God day and night as I come before His throne of grace.

I am going to pray against the accuser that has my blessings backed up. Show me, Lord, the motion of discovery that I may fight my case with the blood of Jesus. Hear my plea, hear my cry Lord. I shall appeal my case before Your courts.

PRISCILLA L. ROSE

I am not going to let the enemy win: my book shall be fulfilled, and I shall walk in my destiny with my hands lifted up and my mouth full of praise.

I am coming out of that place called stuck.

~ Amen

FROM ME TO YOU: THE SONG OF MY SALVATION

PRISCILLA L. ROSE

8 Hide Me Lord

I will say of the Lord, He is my refuge and my fortress: my God; in Him will I trust. He shall cover thee with his feathers, and under his wings shalt thou trust: his truth shall be thy shield and buckler.
Psalms 91:2, 4

You are my hiding place, Lord. There is no other place I would rather be: this is my prayer and supplication to You.

I am crying out in despair and wanting Your help and guidance. So, as I cry out for Your help, hide me, oh Lord. Do not let the enemy overtake me.

As I pray, I'm looking and pondering over those things that I face. Lord, I know you got me! No terror by night, nor arrow that flieth by day can penetrate me and cause me to fall.

"Hide me, oh Lord!" is my supplication. No mountain or valley can keep me from reaching the heights in You that have been destined for me.

Hide me, oh Lord! You are my refuge. You keep me from the torturous winds and wrenching rains; for there is no other place I want to be.

Yes, You are my stronghold, my fortress. Nothing can come between us. I shall stay hidden in You. I shall absorb the oils of Your feathers and trust in You.

Anoint me, oh Lord, for your glory. Let me continue to find grace in Your sight. Grace me, oh Lord, for this journey to come, so that

FROM ME TO YOU: THE SONG OF MY SALVATION

I will not be overtaken by the cares of this life.

Hide me, oh Lord! I shall trust and honor You in everything I do and say. For You have taught me humility and meekness: in You will I trust.

Yes, I am forever grateful for this place that you have brought me to: above and not beneath; the head and not the tail.

Hide me, oh Lord! As you did your servant Moses, hide me in the clift of the rock that I may inundate the weight of your Glory.

Hide me, oh Lord!

~ Amen

PRISCILLA L. ROSE

FROM ME TO YOU: THE SONG OF MY SALVATION

9 What Chocolate Did You Choose?

And Jesus answered and said unto her, Martha, Martha thou art careful and troubled about many things: But one thing is needful: and Mary hath chosen that good part, which shall not be taken away from her

   Luke 10:41-42 KJV

There is a line in the movie Forrest Gump: "Life is like a box of chocolates: you never know what you're going to get." This is so true to the very core of the saying; but, you know what: I choose Jesus – nothing else will do.

This is the attitude Mary had when given the opportunity to sit at the feet of Jesus and glean. Mary knew what was more important at that set time and place. She knew what she needed and she was not letting anything move her from His presence.

This should be your attitude towards the things of Christ: humbling yourself and receiving what He has for you.

We take for granted the freedom we have to worship Christ and serve Him. We do not have to sneak around and hide to read the word of God or pray to our Lord. We do not have to look over our shoulders waiting for the police to come beating our doors down and take our bibles away.

We have to consider the cost and value the time we have with the Lord, putting away those things that occupy our time and hold no value.

Mary knew the value of sitting at the feet of Jesus and listening to

PRISCILLA L. ROSE

His teachings and parables. She knew what wisdom He had to encourage her heart to continue. This oil was so important to her that she neglected the fact that she was one of the hosts. And, by tradition, she should have been serving the men of God.

We, as people of God, have to learn the value of the word of God and not be so occupied with doing things that can wait.

Martha could have waited until after Jesus left to finish whatever task she was so busy doing. Sad to say, she did not realize what she had right there in front of her until it was too late. I would say she missed it.

Do not get so busy and occupied at doing nothing until you miss the mark. Choose the one who can save you, cleanse you and make you whole.

I choose Jesus. What about you?

~ Amen

FROM ME TO YOU: THE SONG OF MY SALVATION

PRISCILLA L. ROSE

10 So Why Did You Eat The Fruit?

And when the woman saw that the tree was good for food, and that it was pleasant to the eyes, and a tree to be desired to make one wise, she took of the fruit thereof, and did eat, and gave also unto her husband with her; and he did eat. And the eyes of them both were opened, and they knew that they were naked; and they sewed fig leaves together, and made themselves aprons.
                                                Genesis 3:6-7 KJV

In life there are boundaries that should not be crossed, and certain roads that need not to be walked down. I believe the old saying is that *curiosity killed the cat*.

All things are not expedient. Have patience and let the Lord work out situations in your life that you cannot handle. Do not be so quick to move on impulse or on your emotions. Seek the Lord for answers and wait until He releases the answers.

As humans, we are quick to move on a feeling or desire and want for something that, at that time, God says not yet. We move ahead of His timing and make a shipwreck of situations because we are blinded by flesh.

For some reason, we do not look and think far ahead of the situation. We get tunnel vision. This is where the enemy has you and wants you to partially see what the ending results will be; not discerning time or reason for the season that you are in.

I do believe if Adam and Eve would have truly understood and foresaw what was ahead, they would not have been so quick to eat from the tree of good and evil. They would have just walked away from the pressure of Satan.

FROM ME TO YOU: THE SONG OF MY SALVATION

They both were open to be tempted. Adam stood by and watched, heard and also gave consent instead of walking away from what was being offered.

Once you feel yourself or your marriage in a rut, do not give the devil any wiggle room. Seek the Lord for guidance. Go to your spouse and discuss how you feel or what you are going through no matter how crazy it may sound; because, if you stay there, the devil will start playing on your emotions and make you feel like you are an island.

While satan is distracting you and playing mind games with you, unknowingly you invite spirits in your home and space. So, you have to be watchful because this may lead to sex outside of your marriage or you slipping up and going back to what you have been delivered from.

Do not be like the young king who took counsel from an unwise generation. Get around seasoned saints who are prayed up; and remember, just because it looks good does not mean it is good for you.

Do not eat the fruit!

~ Amen

PRISCILLA L. ROSE

FROM ME TO YOU: THE SONG OF MY SALVATION

Saved And Satisfied

Saved and satisfied
I might say
Like my favorite fruit because I'm on display

Saved and satisfied
That is what I got to say
It's all good for the rest of my days

Saved and satisfied
I'm gone need you to recognize
For the cost was not easy
So stop being cheesy

Yes! Saved and satisfied
I have no room for the lies

Saved and satisfied
Flesh, you gone have to die
So my spirit can fly

Saved and satisfied

PRISCILLA L. ROSE

Yes everything is alright
Because this ole girl is sanctified, justified
Saved and satisfied

~Amen!

FROM ME TO YOU: THE SONG OF MY SALVATION

PRISCILLA L. ROSE

FROM ME TO YOU: THE SONG OF MY SALVATION

Chapter 3

And My Eyes Shall See
(Faith)

11. *What Do You See?*   44

12. *Watchman! Watchman! What Does The Lord Say?*   47

13. *In That Order*   50

14. *Roll Call Please*   53

15. *When Your Back Is Up Against The Wall*   56

Poem: Dusty Road   59

PRISCILLA L. ROSE

FROM ME TO YOU: THE SONG OF MY SALVATION

11 *What Do You See?*

Glory to God, I see my future, my purpose, and my new me coming into view! I'm walking and talking as I am led by your Holy Spirit. I feel the new me, the authentic me who my Father created me to be.

Yes, Priscilla. But, what do you see?

I see a lady of virtue, a woman of wisdom, and most importantly, a praying vessel. A mother of two with love for many; praying that they find their hope in Christ Jesus.

That's good and all: But, what do you see???

No more lackadaisical because there is work to do. Looking out, I see the blindness the enemy has put over our men's eyes; the loss of respect for one's self and heritage. I see so many of our young women who have walked away from their babies, not realizing that the enemy is waiting and ready to destroy and deploy them.

So, what else do you see?

I see famine and destruction in the land; people walking away from their marriage and families, trying to find an easier way.

I see unrest and division; no honor and justice being served. Sickness and death is walking amongst us, moving people out of the way.

So, what else do you see?

The earth is crying out, waiting for the Saints to take their place. Oh, such a cry in my belly!

PRISCILLA L. ROSE

The Father is looking for hearts of repentance to get it right.
Mercy, Mercy, Mercy I cry out!

I know we hear this over and over again, but it is praying time. Yes, I call each one of you out. Go before God and cry out for our fathers, mothers, sons and daughters. This is the mandate for this time and season that we are in right now.

There are nations that need reviving; government that needs a godly turn around. The people have become lost within their own vanities and self-made ways.

So, our prayers should be that they come out and be saved and set free from the bondage and spell of witchcraft that has formed over their eyes, minds and hearts.

*So, what do **you** see?*

~ Amen

FROM ME TO YOU: THE SONG OF MY SALVATION

12 Watchman! Watchman! What Does The Lord Say?

I will stand upon my watch, and set me upon the tower, and will watch to see what he will say unto me, and what I shall answer when I am reproved.
Habakkuk 2:1 KJV

Waiting on an answer from God is very tedious, but yet intriguing to hear from our heavenly Father.

We don't want to get so pompous and prideful to think He will answer us right away. We are all His and have some level of communication with Him that grows in time.

Like Daniel prayed for an answer concerning the children of Israel and the answer had already come, but the enemy held it up. Trust and believe it is already done and answered in the spiritual realm; but, it may not be time for it to be released. Just remember to stay on the wall with your prayers and supplications.

Everyone that you feel is ready for change spiritually may not be there yet. Some people do not mind staying where they are. So, even though the word or instructions have been released, everyone individually needs to catch it and move forward. This is the parable of the wheat and the tare growing together. So, no matter what, complete your assignment as a watchman.

And, as the Holy Spirit gives you instructions, do not go beyond what He reveals to you on what to say and do; otherwise, you will be working in flesh.

FROM ME TO YOU: THE SONG OF MY SALVATION

I know it can be hard to not be *extra*. But, remember obedience is very important. As you saw in King Saul's situation: because he did not follow instructions, more than once I might add, he was removed from his office.

I will say this once again - stay encouraged and do not be afraid to put before God your inner short comings. These are the little foxes that will kill the vine in you and put you behind on your assignment and where you should be spiritually.

So, let the Holy Spirit reprove you and correct in you what needs to be corrected.

He is the watchman of your soul. So watchman, watchman, what do *you* say?

~ Amen

PRISCILLA L. ROSE

FROM ME TO YOU: THE SONG OF MY SALVATION

13 #InThatOrder

For thou art my lamp, O Lord: and the Lord will lighten my darkness. For by thee I have run through a troop: by my God have I leaped over a wall.
2 Samuel 22:29-30

There are so many obstacles we face in life and walls that will try to block our way. But see, you have to imagine in your mind and get in your spirit that it is coming down.

Imagine yourself kicking the obstacles and walls in with all your strength and power; getting the momentum and will to say to the devil *"That is enough! I am not taking this anymore."*

Remind yourself that the negative voice of rejection is what is speaking in your head; and because you have Christ, you are greater.

You are greater than any situation and circumstance that comes your way; and you are a city that cannot and will not be hid.

Let the enemy know, "Yes, His Holy Spirit resides in me and covers me wherever I go." For it is a small thing for our great God to allow us to conquer our unbelief.

He will guide your hands and word your mouth with praises of victory. Give Him your dance in advance; for it is already done in heaven. For His joy will carry you through your low times, picking you up in your time of sorrow and grief.

For darkness cannot and will never understand the brightness of His light and love He has for you.

PRISCILLA L. ROSE

Grab hold of His word and embrace it in your heart. Do not let the enemy snatch it from you. Let it carry you through your good and bad days; for He will allow His angels to go before you.

So, declare it and decree it that He is the God of your salvation and fear is not welcomed in your life. So, rejoice and be glad that the Lord of your soul favors you and will always see you through.

Lift up your head and stand tall in Christ, knowing He is leading the way and carrying you.

Leap, I say! Leap with a pep in your step, knowing that you are loved by God – #*In That Order*.

~Amen

FROM ME TO YOU: THE SONG OF MY SALVATION

PRISCILLA L. ROSE

14 Roll Call Please

These be the names of the mighty men whom David had: The Tachmonite that sat in the seat, chief among the captains; the same was Adino the Eznite: he lift up his spear against eight hundred, whom he slew at one time.
                                                2 Samuel 23:8KJV

Could you imagine sitting amongst these mighty men, with a king that had the same warrior yet humble spirit; full of wisdom but yet feared God and ruled the kingdom with honor and humility and the mindset of *"I'm yet a man?"*

It just fascinates me how we let the devil hit us upside our heads and snatch or rob our identity, and shake hands with him within the next minute. Acting as though everything is ok in your life and family, when the devil has won too many rounds of this match of life.

David was in the field with the sheep and earning his props, while learning his skills of war and defending his flock. So when the appointed time came for him to be revealed, he won the war for all the children of Israel. He was not pompous and it was not for show. It was his faith in the God of Israel that allowed him to conquer Goliath.

Fear has no friends, but a warrior will be loved among his. Are you among the mighty? Mighty to pray, mighty to love and mighty to go when God sends you? Will your name be on that list in heaven of the mighty for Christ. Every weakness or struggle is a giant in your life; and, if so, it will control your life. You have to make up in your mind and heart that you will not be pulled away from Christ and the things that are holy and righteous.

FROM ME TO YOU: THE SONG OF MY SALVATION

These mighty men's names went in the book and their lineage of the tribe they came from was named with them.

What an honor! Roll call please.

~ Amen

PRISCILLA L. ROSE

FROM ME TO YOU: THE SONG OF MY SALVATION

15 *When Your Back Is Up Against The Wall*

And the sun stood still, and the moon stayed, until the people had avenged themselves upon their enemies. Is not this written in the book of Jasher? So the sun stood still in the midst of heaven, and hasted not to go down about a whole day.
                                        Joshua 10:13 (KJV)

And there was no day like that before it or after it: won't He do it!

My God your God is so faithful and just in all his ways. He tells us that He will make our enemies our footstool and prepare a table before them. However, the catch is to hold your peace and let the Lord fight for you. They may come at you one way; but, He will make sure they flee before you seven ways.

Keep in mind and remember that we are the apple of God's eye; and He loves us and enjoys it when we praise and worship Him. He is our Fortress and Protector. So, when He sees our enemy coming at us, He will fight our battle. For vengeance is His, and we must take Him at His word and let Him lead the way.

Joshua and the children of Israel did not consult God on a certain matter; and, in the end, they had to fight and defend what they took on because of the oath they made with the Gibeons.

Is not that like a loving father looking past your mistakes and still willing to take care of the situation. God could have turned His back on Joshua and the children of Israel; but, because He understood Joshua's heart and the oath he made God, He had his back.

Could you image that battle? Picture in your mind the day not ending and you are out on the field fighting. I am tired just thinking about the intensity of that day. It probably did not resonate in the people's mind what happened until it was too late.

But, that is just like your enemy: they feel that not getting a reaction from you means you are weak.

Think about it. You are in battle, and out of nowhere hailstones start coming from heaven. Or the sun never goes down and the moon never appears. My God, what a day!

As always, God shows up no matter what the accuser tries to accuse us of. He will keep us from the arrows that fly by day and the terror by night. As long as our faith is in Him and not in man, He will cover us and keep His hedge of protection around us.

Remember to never let the enemy knock you off of "your square" and put you in a situation that you would regret. Quickly repent and apologize; and do not let your pride and stubbornness keep you from getting it right.

God will take care of those that are coming against you and shut the mouth of your enemy. It is not what they do, but it is how you respond and your accountability to Christ.

So, when your back is against the wall, trust God – He will come through.

~ Amen

FROM ME TO YOU: THE SONG OF MY SALVATION

PRISCILLA L. ROSE

Dusty Road

Is that zeal at the starting line
Praying that you made it right on time
Not having to stand in line

Looking down you realize
Winding roads you shall find
Contemplating on looking behind
Figuring out there's nothing to find

Walk that dusty road
Feel the rays drumming on your soul

Walk that dusty road
I tell you there's no mirage on that road

Walk that dusty road
Can you feel the pebbles on the bottom of your soles

Walk that dusty road
Cause there's life at the end of the road

FROM ME TO YOU: THE SONG OF MY SALVATION

PRISCILLA L. ROSE

FROM ME TO YOU: THE SONG OF MY SALVATION

Chapter 4
Made Up Mind

(Value)

16. My First I Shall Abide   64

17. Hidden Figure   67

18. Beauty For Ashes   70

19. Found Treasure   73

20. He Keeps His Promises   76

Poem: Yes This Is For His Glory   80

PRISCILLA L. ROSE

FROM ME TO YOU: THE SONG OF MY SALVATION

16 *My First I Shall Abide*

Paul said to the centurion and to the soldiers, Except these abide in the ship, ye cannot be saved.
Acts 27:31 KJV

It's so awesome how God strategically sets up different events and brings order into our life to remind us that nothing happens by chance. Paul was given the warning; yet, he was still pressed in the spirit to go ahead and go.

Wow! He knew part of the outcome; but, he still wanted to go, regardless of what the angel revealed to him.

Yes, he was bound in chains and in prison; yet, God covered him and showed him favor through the process.

Paul knew his assignment. Do we know and understand our assignment? Is our ear attentive and listening for instructions that the Holy Spirit is giving us? Are we spreading the good news of Jesus Christ?

People, we have to realize that it is all about those that are lost and feel that there is no hope; those that feel that they are trapped in their addictions and mental handicaps and feel they have no way of escape. We have to remind them to push and press toward their freedom and not give in.

Yes, you have to let some people go that you are connected to in order to get back in your God-given purpose.

So many people in the world are searching for their identities while

PRISCILLA L. ROSE

believing the lies of the devil. But, God is searching for those that are willing to pick up their cross and walk along side His Son; showing love and compassion – letting everyone know He has risen with all power. For greater works is what is required of us.

We have to get back to our first love, which is Christ Jesus, and not allow this world to change us; but, letting everyone see that there is a difference between the clean and unclean.

Righteousness and holiness is still our Father's mandate for our lives. Yes, some will make it on boards and broken pieces; but, the thing is, you made it.

You do not have to be the greatest or most eloquent speaker in the world. It is your heart that is most important. God searches the intent of your heart and motive behind it. What is driving you? Are you a soul-ish person moving in flesh; or, are you spirit-led.

He wants to know can He trust you with His people. Can you lead them to Him and His righteousness by His word?

So, I would say, Come and abide in the ship, and do not miss out on what He has in store for you for there is safety in Christ Jesus.

~ Amen

FROM ME TO YOU: THE SONG OF MY SALVATION

PRISCILLA L. ROSE

17 Hidden Figure

And there was one Anna, a prophetess, the daughter of Phanuel, of the tribe of Asher: but served God with fasting and prayers night and day. And she coming in that instant gave thanks likewise unto the Lord, and spake of him to all them that looked for redemption in Jerusalem.
Luke 2:36a, 37c, 38 (KJV)

The most powerful and anointed men and women of God are those that are in the background not trying to be seen or recognized for what they do for the Kingdom of God.

They deposit prayers and fasting on behalf of others, interceding for families and strangers who they may never meet.

As for Anna, I believe she was one of the ones that prayed a prayer of warfare on behalf of Christ to be delivered out of the hands of the enemy. I believe she waged war in the spiritual realm to make sure Mary and Joseph were covered and no harm to be done to them. Remember, she was a woman of prayer and fasting night and day.

It tells us in Isaiah that fasting will loose the bands of wickedness to undo the heavy burdens, and to let the oppressed go free, and that you will be strengthened to break every yoke. This is the life Anna lived; and, we as men and women of God should duplicate this example of living for our lives today.

There was little said about Anna the prophetess, but what was said holds a lot of weight. If you can sustain yourself and be kept for 84 years while working in the temple of the Lord, that shows us

FROM ME TO YOU: THE SONG OF MY SALVATION

that we have no excuses. She was a happy and blessed woman of God who did not let her riches come before her time with the Lord.

Anna was excited and made plenty of room for the things of God. She directed people's attention to the importance of Christ being born. This should be a great impingement to us now, here in today's society.

The Lord should always be the main equation and conversation in of our life no matter how much money we have or what status we achieve. For it is him that allows the blessings to be upon us and our families.

Keep in mind, being hidden is not the end of a thing; it is the continuation of the matter of Kingdom work.

~ Amen

PRISCILLA L. ROSE

FROM ME TO YOU: THE SONG OF MY SALVATION

18 *Beauty for Ashes*

To appoint unto them that mourn in Zion, to give unto them beauty for ashes, the oil of joy for mourning, the garment of praise for the spirit of heaviness; that they might be called trees of righteousness, the planting of the Lord, that he might be glorified.
Isaiah 61:3 (KJV)

I will trust in and believe God's promises for I am part of the evidence that freedom is real. My praise cannot be taken away, and I believe in the report of the Lord. I am no longer a broken woman any more.

There are a lot of things that can hold a person back from fulfilling one's purpose. One reason is fear; another is lack of confidence.

Consequently, this could come from one's childhood, from being abandoned by one or both parents. Additionally, it could be a generational curse, either started by you or your parents or grandparents. Just know the enemy lies in wait for an entry point; and, once he gets it, he will try to get full access.

This is why it is so important to teach your children about Jesus Christ so that they may have a foundation.

We cannot give the devil leeway. We have to stop him in his tracks and close the door on his accusations for he has no legal rights over us. We were bought with a price; therefore, we are not our own but God's.

So, confess this over your life: *"My hands, feet, mouth, lips, soul and spirit shall obey God through my worship and praise."*

PRISCILLA L. ROSE

This is our reasonable service to God for allowing us to breathe His air and behold the beauty of life

No, things are not always going to be easy, and freedom does have a price. Yes, we may get trapped in a hurting and confused lifestyle. Additionally, your soul may have picked up bad habits as you travelled through life's journey; or, you may have been mishandled as a child.

Moreover, circumstances like these can make you become bitter and angry; full of perversion and hurt from the damage that was done to your soul. It also can make you become emotionless and numb from what life has handed you.

I believe there is a saying that goes like this: If you know to do right, then do right. But, that saying does not always register when you are in sin; it does not click mentally until you accept Christ.

This is how the devil works: He will make you go against the grain, lose your identity and fall behind in your life's purpose and destiny. But, let us not forget that our heavenly Father *is* time and can restore what the locust and the cankerworm, and caterpillar and palmerworm have destroyed by eating up your harvest.

This could show up in your finances, children, job and the right doors being opened.

See, this is what the devil is after. All of this is connected to your peace of mind; knowing that your provisions in life are taken care of.

Your mind has to be set that God is *your* everything. We must be

FROM ME TO YOU: THE SONG OF MY SALVATION

like a tree with the stance that the only way I'm coming down is to be cut down. I'm going to be rooted and grounded in Christ.

This outside beauty is temporal and it will not last forever.

Say it out loud: *"Lord, work on my inner man!"* For your fruit will surely spring forth and bear witness that God will reward those who diligently seek Him.

So, I say to you are you ready to trade your beauty for ashes? For beauty is only skin deep. But, it is the inner person that will attract God and the right people in your life.

~ Amen

PRISCILLA L. ROSE

FROM ME TO YOU: THE SONG OF MY SALVATION

19 Found Treasure

You have taken account of my wanderings; Put my tears in your bottle. Are they not recorded in your book?
Psalms 56:8 (Amp)

As the days and years go by, I find myself sitting here wondering why I have not been found. Looking at myself and analyzing my wealth, there is no reason why.

You see, I look around me, and I see others that shine in their own unique way. Some may sparkle, some may glisten; but it is not the looks that uphold the value of the matter.

Buried away and hiding underneath my own flaws; not understanding why I cannot get past these four walls.

Walls of pity. Walls of shame. They seem to have held my name. Rejection, not depression, came looking through the spectacles of my eyes.

Looking over my shoulder I hear a voice say *"You are not worth the time or space: stay in your place. You hold nothing and you came from nothing; please be on your way. There is no room for you, child. Do we need to say it out loud, sweetie? Stay in your place."*

Then something shakes me and awakens me; that call in the cool of the day: My daughter my daughter you mean so much to me. I have made you and shaped you to place you in the hands of the right man. You I have placed in his heart, awaiting for him to do his part; preparing for the start of kingdom work.

PRISCILLA L. ROSE

Favor, you have brought him; now, the closed doors can open because two are better than one.

You have weathered your storms, and strength you have formed to carry on. You shall lift each other up and comfort one another when you're worried because two are better than one.

The heat of the matter does not rely on just one. For Yes, you are that found treasure!

~ Amen

FROM ME TO YOU: THE SONG OF MY SALVATION

PRISCILLA L. ROSE

20 *He Keeps his Promises*

Every good gift and every perfect gift is from above, and cometh down from the Father of lights, with whom is no variableness, neither shadow of turning.
James 1:17 (KJV)

This is what I know and hold on to: my Heavenly Father keeps His word.

There are promises that are told to us by God's written word or revealed in dreams and visions. Some may be delayed for various reason: it could be because of disobedience, or the enemy is trying to hold up or block your blessings.

But, you have to remember that we walk by faith and not by sight. What the enemy wants us to dwell on is what we do not see with the natural eye.

I encourage you to remind yourself of the word that is written. Or, remember the prophetic dreams or visions He has shown you. Come into agreement with it because only you know your petitions that you have before the Lord.

Also, you will come to understand that through your faithfulness He will bless you. He knows us. He knows what we need. He knows our wants and desires.

Always keep in mind that our Heavenly Father knows what is best when we do not see it or agree with it.

As a seer/prophet, I'm shown quite a few things; but, I have to remind myself that some things may be out of flesh and not

FROM ME TO YOU: THE SONG OF MY SALVATION

spiritual.

If you are unsure, pray and ask the Lord for revelation and confirmation. If you have to fast, do so as well. Do not be ashamed; this is between you and the Father. Everyone gets discouraged. Even Moses, when dealing with the children of Israel, got discouraged; but, he still was mentioned in the walk of faith scriptures.

If you look at the scripture in James, it says: *with Whom is no variableness*. He will not waiver or change his mind; and, He most definitely is not fickle in his decisions.

No matter how many days or years may pass, your " it" shall come to pass.

We also may not remember every word that was prophesied to us, or scripture we have read; but, keep in your heart the fact that He will reward those who diligently seek Him.

He will give unto you good measure pressed down, shaken together and running over (Luke 6:38).And God will meet all your needs according to His riches in glory in Christ Jesus (Phillippians 4:19). After all, blessed is the one who trusts in the Lord.

It is a blessing all by itself to believe in Him and take His word at face value for he is the Spirit of Truth and His promises are yes and amen.

Always remember to keep Christ at the head of your life; and, no matter what, He is there for you.

Whither shall I go from thy spirit? Or, whither shall I flee from thy presence? If I ascend up into heaven, thou art there: if I

PRISCILLA L. ROSE

make my bed in hell, behold, thou art there.(Psalms 139:7-8).

He is here. Whatever your decisions in life – whether He agrees or not – He will help you through it.

Remember that God does not get excited when we mess up; but, He is patient with us. So, be patient with Him for He always keeps His promises.

Fulfilling His promises is God's way of telling His children that you are more than just the dirt from which I made you. But, it is me looking at me in a mirror. For out of my grace you came, and out of my mercy I allowed you to continue at your own free will.

God loves us and He wants the best for His own.

Thank you for keeping Your promises!

~ Amen

FROM ME TO YOU: THE SONG OF MY SALVATION

PRISCILLA L. ROSE

Yes, This Is For His Glory!

I've been preserved, positioned and established for his Glory!
Maintained and groomed for His use only.
Yes I stayed and prayed for His hand to make and mold me,
and not fold me, into a subject that has no point or purpose...
Yes this is for his Glory!

For I see myself climbing higher and higher –
to the mountaintop I go.
One step at a time with no *fitbits* to elaborate on a subject that only He knows...
Yes this is for his Glory!

I've kept my stride, leaving those things behind
that weighed me down and shoved me around
Yes this is for his Glory!

My heart is fixed, my mind is made up
No turning back to the old P who wore it proudly on her chest...
Yes this is for his Glory!

The smell is gone, the stench has passed;
sin is no longer my hold...
Yes this is for his Glory!

FROM ME TO YOU: THE SONG OF MY SALVATION

Kept, I say; preserved I say for that day...
Yes this is for his Glory!

Lord over my soul, Jealous of my foes that had me
and grabbed me and dragged me to that one way road...
Yes this is for his Glory!

I'm not moving. I'm not budging.
Faith has captured me and established me...
Yes this is for his Glory!

A love I can't explain
For shame no longer holds my name...
Yes this is for his Glory!

PRISCILLA L. ROSE

FROM ME TO YOU: THE SONG OF MY SALVATION

PRISCILLA L. ROSE

Chapter 5
It's Mine
(Joy)

21. *Follow The Breadcrumbs*   *87*

22. *The Clean Up Is Real*   *90*

23. *So Fresh So Clean*   *93*

24. *Perfection We Go*   *97*

25. *Going For Broke*   *101*

Poem: Looking Beyond That Mountain   *104*

FROM ME TO YOU: THE SONG OF MY SALVATION

PRISCILLA L. ROSE

21 Follow The Bread Crumbs

And when the woman saw that she was not hid, she came trembling, and falling down before him, she declared unto him before all the people for what cause she had touched him, and how she was healed immediately. And he said unto her, Daughter be of good comfort: thy faith hath made thee whole; go in peace.
Luke 8:47-48 (KJV)

Could you imagine the night before in your bed laying there not being able to sleep in anticipation of meeting Jehovah Rapha in the flesh?

Hearing all the testimonies of everyone else being healed, but you are still in the same state. Going from one doctor to another and getting no results.

Could you imagine dreaming of what it would be for the problem you have had to deal with year after year for twelve years, finally coming to an end?

Seeing yourself coming up to the crowd, and moving through the people inch by inch. Passing by those whom He has already touched and healed, and are now rejoicing over their healing; but, you have not got to Him yet.

Contemplating and questioning in your mind *"Will he heal me or reject me?"*

Could you imagine people bumping into you, shoving you, and trying to move you out of their way to make it to the Messiah?

FROM ME TO YOU: THE SONG OF MY SALVATION

Deep down in your heart, you know by law you are not supposed to be there without yelling out and let it be known that you are unclean: *I am an unclean woman!"*

But, you are rationalizing in your heart at this time and moment that none of that matters; not despondency or dreariness. Yet being determined, you say *"I am going to make it through and break through this crowd and get my healing."*

It is a beautiful thing when you hear the testimonies of others who went through the same situation and problem that you are going through in your health and life.

Finding out the ending results came from the Holy Spirit moving either in a service or prayers that went up to heaven. These are "breadcrumbs" – things we can pick up and follow and eat on.

Keep in mind that there are always witnesses to what Christ has done, then and now. God is the same today, yesterday and forever; He never changes.

Everything is done for His Glory, no matter what the end results may be. The doctors may say one thing, but God has the final say.

Get Your Healing and follow the breadcrumbs.

~ Amen

PRISCILLA L. ROSE

FROM ME TO YOU: THE SONG OF MY SALVATION

22 The Clean Up Is Real

Then he saith, I will return into my house from whence I came out; and when he is come, he findeth it empty, swept, and garnished. Then goeth he, and taketh with himself seven other spirits more wicked than himself, and they enter in and dwell there: and the last state of that man is worse than the first. Even so shall it be also unto this wicked generation.
Matthew 12:44-45

Deliverance is the children's bread. But, the Holy Spirit, at His will, can impart it to whom He please, if they sincerely want to be free.

Deliverance is nothing to be played with: once you are free from that stronghold, replace it with the word of God. Do not go back to what he freed you from. Do not look for it, or try to figure out what it was. Just walk in your victory.

It truly is an honor and a privilege for the Lord to grant us His Grace of deliverance in our lives, and untangle the webs we put ourselves in. His grace is something that we should not take lightly.

Remember this is one of the great reasons Christ gave His life for us: to redeem us back to our Father and be able to come before His throne of grace.

Deliverance is like cleaning your house. It is an everyday task to make sure the dust and dirt is kept at a minimum.

This reward you cannot let the devil steal from you. You truly have to guard it with your breastplate of righteousness and helmet

PRISCILLA L. ROSE

of salvation.

Definitely recognize your own demons. Recognize what He brought you out of. They are coming; but, when they come, make sure there is no space for them.

There is a scripture in Colossians that tells us to touch not, taste not, and handle not. If you stay mindful of this in your day to day life, it will keep you from your old, bad habits.

So, remember whom the Son sets free is free indeed: keep this in your heart, because the cleanup is real!

~ Amen

FROM ME TO YOU: THE SONG OF MY SALVATION

PRISCILLA L. ROSE

23 So Fresh! So Clean!

Then will I sprinkle clean water upon you, and ye shall be clean: from all your filthiness, and from all your idols, will I cleanse you. A new heart also will I give you, and a new spirit will I put within you: and I will take away the stony heart out of your flesh, and I will give you a heart of flesh.
Ezekiel 36:25-26(KJV)

I love you Lord for seeing me and looking past my shortcomings, and forgiving me. No matter what I do not see, He sees and continues to operate on me.

The hand of the Lord is always in operation mode and in transformation drive. Whether it is in slow motion, or He is moving in fast acceleration, He is constantly working on or in us to get us to the place where we can be most effectively used.

It is so important to stay in a position of humility and open to what the Holy Spirit wants to do in us.

Keep in mind to always have a "Yes" in your heart, whether you understand what He is doing or not. Sometimes we can be our own worst enemy by blocking what He wants to do through us and in us. This is called self sabotage.

One thing I have learned in this walk in Christ is that "Yes!" is a very important word. It should always be Yes to His will, Yes to His righteousness, and Yes to His holiness. To get there, you have to have a made up mind and a yielded heart. It cannot just be lip service and moving in your emotions. It has to come from the belly; the depths of your soul crying out for help.

FROM ME TO YOU: THE SONG OF MY SALVATION

Just as a heart surgeon washes the heart and prepares it before he places it in the patient, God does just the same.

We all go through seasons of washing and healing; but, if there is a spirit blocking this, He will take you through a time of straight deliverance.

And, Yes you have to be honest with God and with yourself about what you are dealing with in your soul. When you come clean with your Heavenly Father, then He will make you clean.

There is nothing more peaceful than feeling freedom in your mind and soul from the things that have had you bound! Freedom from things like depression, oppression, perversion, lying and stealing; these are only a few.

So, as saints, let us keep our hearts ready and our minds made up that we want to be changed over. We want to be in that number that made it through great tribulation with our robes washed in the blood and made white as snow.

That stony heart is a dark heart that is heavy and stubborn; full of unforgiveness and bitterness while looking at what others have done and not what you have dished out.

Be accountable for yourself and what you have done. The easy way out is to point the finger at everyone else. But, look back and analyze it again. See it through the eyes of Christ and not your eyes that need to be purged.

So, let us get it in order and let God operate on us, making us clean

PRISCILLA L. ROSE

and renewed; ready to love and obey His word.

So fresh! So clean!

~ Amen

FROM ME TO YOU: THE SONG OF MY SALVATION

PRISCILLA L. ROSE

24 *2 PerfectiOn We Go!*

Therefore let us get past the elementary stage in the teachings about the Christ, advancing on to maturity and perfection and spiritual completeness, [doing this] without laying again a foundation of repentance from dead works and of faith toward God.
Hebrews 6:1 (AMP)

I desire to sit at a supper table where the table is spread with plenty to eat and plenty of leftovers. Where we all can sit and enjoy the fruit of our hands and the joy in our hearts in preparing the feast.

The word of God is the preparation of the meal for the people and yourself. Everything has an ingredient or formula for your consumption, or for other uses.

Let us take mashed potatoes that can be consumed by babies and adults. It is either thick or smooth. To me that is how the word should be taught; not over everyone's head; but, simple enough that even the babies in Christ can come and eat as well.

We want to come to a place where we can feel the growth and maturity in the Holy Spirit. We should not allow the same things to get to us year after year.

Consequently, we should be praying for those who vex us or misuse and abuse our kindness.

Love and forgiveness are elementary things when we speak and teach about Christ. But yet, this is the hardest test for us as saints.

FROM ME TO YOU: THE SONG OF MY SALVATION

They are not just words and should not be easily thrown around. It should be action behind them.

Nevertheless, somehow things that people go through in life hinders them from reaching this maturity.

We cannot let rape, molestation, abuse or misuse keep us from being used by God. If we allow the enemy to hover this over our heads and torment us, we let him win.

Maturity is the state or quality of being mature; a change of mindset and life goals in the spirit. Not letting our emotions rule our thoughts and life, but lining up our mind, spirit and soul with the word of God. Not letting our response be through hurting eyes and ears.

The Lord will perfect those things concerning you if you move your emotions and flesh out of the way and allow the Holy Spirit to lead you.

The Lord is patient and merciful. He is not going to throw you to the wolves. He will see you through. He is a father that looks after His children by comforting them and counseling them. You cannot let the situation be louder than God's voice.

Perfection – the state or condition of being perfect; freedom from fault or defect; maturity; supreme excellence; the act or process of perfecting. This is what the Holy Spirit wants us to accomplish in him through his guidance.

It starts with the mindset of the person; to have faith and believe that this can be done and you can make it through every test and trial.

PRISCILLA L. ROSE

Consequently, after every test comes power and more of His anointing upon your life.

Blessed are you who endureth the temptations of life for they come to make you strong. This is part of your maturity in Christ.

Please remember your hands are made to war and heal God's people; and not steal. Your mouth was made to cry out and spare; lifting up your voice to the Lord in song and praise; not to swear and curse people. Your body was made to be a temple for the Holy Ghost; not to destroy it with alcohol, drugs, tobacco and uncovenant relationships.

And, not to be given over to the spirit of heathenism with tattoos, piercings and markings; cutting of the flesh. We are no longer bound to the spirit of being heathens once we come into the knowledge of the true and living God.

Not worshipping strange idols, deity gods and pagan festivities; putting it before God and His principles.

Finally, let us keep moving toward perfection and spiritual completeness in Christ. Spiritual completeness is having all the necessary parts [tools], not lacking anything. Not limited in any way; not requiring more work. It is entirely done or completed.

This is the work of Christ Jesus by ways and means of God's Holy Spirit working through us. All tools and essentials are there: we just have to grab hold of them, move forward and grow in Christ to do a work in the kingdom.

To perfection we go.

~ Amen

FROM ME TO YOU: THE SONG OF MY SALVATION

PRISCILLA L. ROSE

25 Going For Broke

Then Paul answered, What mean you to weep and to break mine heart? For I am ready not to be bound only, but also to die at Jerusalem for the name of the Lord Jesus.
Acts 21:13(KJV)

When professing Christ, there are going to be a lot of oppositions coming at you because of your faith.

Paul knew the challenges ahead of him, but he did not let this deter him from his assignment.

This, people of the most high, has to be our same posture when it comes to the things of Christ. Yes, the enemy will try to hold up finances and close doors; but remember, if God be for us, who can be against us.

You ever wonder why certain people just do not like you, or say it is just something about her or him? Well, it is because of the life you have chosen; a life of righteousness and holiness where favor follows you no matter what door you walk through literally. It is like jealousy smells you out and waits for you to walk through the door.

At times, we forget that longsuffering comes along with following Christ, and He has to keep our flesh of retaliation in check.

We are quick to point out what the other person has done to us; but, God is looking at your response in the situation. Do not let the enemy kill you before your assignment has been completed. Repent and go through the test again. Rest assured that you are going to have to do a repeat of that course, either with that same

FROM ME TO YOU: THE SONG OF MY SALVATION

person or someone else until you pass the test.

Go for broke for Christ because the end results will be beyond what you can even imagine.

As people of the world, we went hard for the devil – partying and living it up, we thought.

Flip that and do the same for Christ: give Him your all, because He gave, and continues to give to you His all.

For there is no good thing that He will withhold from those who walk upright.

So, go for broke!

~ Amen

PRISCILLA L. ROSE

FROM ME TO YOU: THE SONG OF MY SALVATION

Looking Beyond That Mountain

A pile of dirt and rubble
Built up to block my view.
But I move in closer to see
Because I envy the height and width indeed.

It's taller than me and wider I see.
So I move in closer to help my unbelief.
Noticing the beauty I stop to feel with my hand
I tend to forget the plans.

Distracted by the aroma of the flowers on my level.
I forget the agenda at hand.

Then I hear a still small voice reminding me.
Look beyond the mountain and see.
Back on track I must go.
Climbing higher and higher to the top,
Realizing there is no time to stroll.

The air is thinner but my strength will I commend.
I'm here, you see, not giving in
To unbelief, that yes, it is beyond this mountain:
My future and destiny.

PRISCILLA L. ROSE

So I make it and see that there is plenty for me.
Looking beyond that mountain I know.
God truly has a plan for me.

~ Amen

FROM ME TO YOU: THE SONG OF MY SALVATION

PRISCILLA L. ROSE

FROM ME TO YOU: THE SONG OF MY SALVATION

Chapter 6
Time To Shift
(Levels)

26. *Lead Me From The Dry Brook*   110

27. *Leap Baby Leap*   115

28. *Cross The Finish Line*   119

29. *My Color Of Peace*   122

Poem: No Way Of Return   125

PRISCILLA L. ROSE

FROM ME TO YOU: THE SONG OF MY SALVATION

26 Lead Me From The Dry Brook

1 Kings 17:1-24 (KJV)

There is nothing worse than being in a dry place and not hearing from God; and, everything ceases until He allows you to move. Selah

In our minds, we feel this way; but, in all reality we are always hearing from God. If not, you would not know you were in a dry place. In fact, this is a moment in time where He wants you to figure out if it is Him you want.

Do you want to go higher, or will you give up? Will you press on, or will you blame others for what the devil is trying to push you back into? I pray that turning back is not an option, no matter what is going on.

Elijah the Prophet did not know the elements or the outcome of the spiritual realm when he spoke the words that it would neither dew or rain for three and a half years. All of his focus was on doing the will of God and proving to King Ahab who the true and living God was.

I have learned in life that everything pretty much has a trickle effect on the outcome of different matters and situations. That is why it is so important to stay before God with an ear to hear what He is instructing us to do as ministers of Christ.

If the brook did not dry up, He would not have been led to the widow woman's house.

See, God will put us in a place to feed us and sustain us for a moment and season of our life. But, when it is time to move, we have to be ready.

It simply amazes me how God used a bird that feeds on pretty much anything; but, yet it is one of the most unusually intelligent birds here on earth.

These birds brought him flesh and bread, morning and evening for three and a half years. Follow me when I say this: you can be in a ministry for however many years being fed and flourishing in the levels the Holy Spirit gives you access to. Then, all of a sudden, the Holy Spirit speaks and instructs you to pick up and go and says *"Your next level and assignment is not here: the brook has dried up."*

For you, there may be a famine; but, for others, that ministry might just be their destiny to function and work in.

Now, God didn't send Elijah to a house that had plenty of money and food with servants and cattle. He was sent to a house where there was a need of a miracle and a visitation from God's Prophet to speak a blessing in the house.

You will not always be sent to a place of plenty. Sometimes He will send you to a place of just enough.

When God moves you to your next, it should be fruit to what He has instructed for you to do. What the widow woman had, God increased it and nothing was wasted.

One thing about being a servant of the Lord is the fact that we have to recognize and discern who wants the oil and who does not. We have to ask ourselves if we are willing to sacrifice the time into prayer and fastings. Are we willing to read and study His word?

FROM ME TO YOU: THE SONG OF MY SALVATION

This is what the barrel of meal and the cruse of oil represented: His word of life, and the anointing functioning in us.

Now, Elijah did not realize that God had another plan for him while he was yet at the widow woman's house. One thing about God is He will establish you and He will make room for your gift to draw the unbeliever to Him.

So, I believe the widow woman must still have had doubts in her heart of what God could do because, as soon as her son fell sick and died, she felt that she was the blame from her past sins for what had transpired.

Even Elijah had a *selah* moment and questioned God about the events that were happening.

People of God, there is nothing wrong with questioning God and reminding him of His promises. When you take time and build a relationship with the Lord wholeheartedly, and follow His instructions, He will release the blessings and miracles in your life. But, do not be so quick to judge the matter. Wait patiently and watch Him move in His timing.

God does not hold grudges or wave our past sins in front of our faces while holding back our blessings. He is merciful and just; full of compassion and patient. No respect of persons. He loves and blesses all His children. Our sins are thrown in the depth of the sea; so, do not go fishing to get them out. Leave them there.

My prayer is that, when we come to the place of transition to move forward spiritually and naturally, we are ready and in place.

Our next is also somebody else's next when we walk in obedience and humility.

PRISCILLA L. ROSE

We are not doing ministry – we *are* ministry, walking epistles spreading the good news of Christ.

So, come from the dry brook and get to the place where we are most effective.

Lead me from the dry brook.

~ Amen

FROM ME TO YOU: THE SONG OF MY SALVATION

PRISCILLA L. ROSE

27 Leap Baby Leap!

I can recall the first time I realized I was pregnant with my first born. I had stuffed myself with turnip greens that seemed not to agree with my body, and I had rushed to the bathroom to throw up.

The greens had not settled in my belly, and I guess she did not like them at the time. Also, as I lay on my back in the bed, I could see her in my belly – the little bump. So, there was no more denying that I was 16 and having a baby.

Read Luke 1:41-45

As I read the salutation between two great women of God, I realized the prophetic confirmation Elisabeth gave to her cousin and the ministry that had to be birthed by both women.

WOW! What an awesome and supernatural experience these women had at this moment. It is at these moments we realize that something is about to shift, bring change and impact the kingdom.

It is at these moments that we realize the greatness and purpose the Lord has placed in us that has to be birthed.

Elisabeth was in her 6th month when she came to know Mary was pregnant with our Savior.

Elisabeth was old and barren; but, God saw fit to restore unto her the desires of her heart. It is all about time and season for the generations that we are to impact.

The Lord doesn't look at our age or our title or where we come from.

FROM ME TO YOU: THE SONG OF MY SALVATION

He does not care if you came from an abusive home or was violated by family or neighbors. He wants a yielded and willing heart for only He knows the intent of our hearts. He also knows if we can carry out what He has placed within us.

A woman carries a natural child for nine months; but, when it comes to a spiritual birth, it is up to the Holy Spirit.

We have to go through the process of being made and washed over again to be used by the Holy Spirit. It takes being crushed, pressed and tried to bring us to the point of humility.

For God so loved the world. So, it is not just for those we serve on a daily basis. The gifts and grace for the kingdom has to be birthed.

Every birth is different. Like a woman who has had multiple children, she will tell you a different story for each child. Some were easy to birth, and some difficult to deliver; but, the result is kingdom work.

And blessed is she that believed: for there shall be a performance of those things which were told her from the Lord. (Luke 1:45)

There is one thing to *hear* the word; but, it is different when you believe and exercise your faith in it.

We only know and see in part. It takes a relationship with the Holy Spirit to reveal to us what it is that has to be birthed.

So, I pray, Lord, that, whatever you have placed inside me to be

PRISCILLA L. ROSE

birthed, I do not want to abort; but, deliver in strength and impregnability.

Leap baby leap!

~ Amen

FROM ME TO YOU: THE SONG OF MY SALVATION

PRISCILLA L. ROSE

28 Cross the Finish Line

And Jesus said unto him, No man, having put his hand to the plough, and looking back, is fit for the kingdom of God. (Luke 9:62KJV)

As a disciple of the Lord, we have to keep our priorities straight and excuses to a minimum.

God knows exactly what is in us and what we can accomplish. If we put our hearts into it, worship is simple: worship is your praise, your stance, your using of your gifts and talents that He has blessed you with for the Kingdom.

It only makes sense as Christians that we give back what He blessed us with. If it is to serve, do it with all your might. If it is to teach or preach, do it with conviction and passion.

Remember, the word hits *you* first before He allows you to speak it to others. And, if he commissioned you to be a greeter or listener, do it with love and humility.

Additionally, when you confess Christ as your Lord and Savior, you are giving him access to all of you. Allow the Holy Spirit to guide you into all truth and righteousness, clinging onto the things that are holy.

So, stay focused on what is ahead, letting go of the things that are keeping you from crossing the finish line.

You see, your finish line is not when the Father calls you home; that is only one line. You have many more to cross.

If you have struggles and habits that keep you from moving

FROM ME TO YOU: THE SONG OF MY SALVATION

forward, those are finish lines as well.

So, be prepared: this time is borrowed time and not guaranteed. You are not in competition with anyone but your flesh; and, you have to win.

You see, it does not matter if you have to run, walk or crawl; just make sure you get across that finish line for there are many obstacle courses ahead of you.

A race started and not finished is like a task undone. Keep your hands to the plough and cross that finish line.

~ Amen

PRISCILLA L. ROSE

FROM ME TO YOU: THE SONG OF MY SALVATION

29 My Color Of Peace

Now Israel loved Joseph more than all his children, because he was the son of his old age: and he made him a coat of many colours. And when his brethren saw that their father loved him more than all his brethren, they hated him, and could not speak peaceably unto him.
Genesis 37:3-4 KJV

I have found in life that peace does not come easy if you are out in the world doing you. It takes a lot of time and energy to get to that point; however, you really do not reach that point of peace while in the world. I have found the simplest solution in this equation, and that is Jesus Christ.

Looking at Joseph's life at a young age, he had peace in spite of the negativity he was receiving from his siblings. He overlooked them and continued on as if nothing was going to shift in his life.

The coat of many colours and the love from his father was what he thought was the cause of his peace and that was enough for him.

Even though it was a coat of many colours, it represented honor and rank only worn by chiefs and heirs. So, he wasn't going to let their pettiness bring him down out of his place of peace.

Peace graced him so until, even when he didn't have the coat anymore, he still found favor amongst the Egyptians.

Keep in mind it is not the prayer shawl or prayer blanket; it is not even the prayer room or closet. You can dress it up, or light it up; but, it is you – you are the tabernacle that you must present to the Lord.

PRISCILLA L. ROSE

So, in presenting your vessel to be used as a representation of Christ here on earth, it is where you will find your peace.

Do not look at people and objects for this inner peace. Look towards Christ and grasp and understand His thoughts toward you.

Additionally, in knowing His thoughts which are His will for your life, you will see and understand the benefits in it.

This is not just the natural, but, most importantly, it is the spiritual blessings in it; and that is what we want: God's peace, and for Him to give us an expected end. That is His path that was set before us before the beginning of this world.

So, I admonish you to seek the Lord and His peace so that your soul may prosper in the things of God. This is a cause and effect situation.

In order to receive your abundance here on earth, find your color of peace. I found mine!

Thank You Jesus!

~ Amen

FROM ME TO YOU: THE SONG OF MY SALVATION

PRISCILLA L. ROSE

No Way Of Return!

I Decree and Declare that I am a woman of faith
Full of wisdom and integrity,
And I will uphold my sisters and bear their infirmities
Through their trying times in prayer and fastings.

I Declare that I shall walk in the will of my Heavenly Father
And fulfill my purpose here on this earth
And joyfully walk into my destiny
In which He has set and prepared before me.

I Declare that I will be that mourning and cunning woman of God
To pray and cry out for my family, youth of this world,
The lost and abused, for our communities,
Cities, states and nations and governments.

I Declare that I am that virtuous woman
And not a silly and foolish woman
For I shall build my house on a love for charity
Through a hope in Christ Jesus our solid foundation.

I Declare that I am blessed, blessed in my city,
Blessed in my field of work, blessed in my coming in
And going out of wherever my feet tread.

FROM ME TO YOU: THE SONG OF MY SALVATION

I Declare that, because the Holy Spirit is within me,
He will guide me;
The fragrance of favor is my scent and aroma;
As I sojourn here until my father calls me home.

In Christ Jesus name

~ Amen

PRISCILLA L. ROSE

FROM ME TO YOU: THE SONG OF MY SALVATION

www.ingramcontent.com/pod-product-compliance
Lightning Source LLC
Chambersburg PA
CBHW030259010526
44107CB00053B/1761